Our
Bucket List
Journal

A Journal for Couples

These Adventures Belong To

_____ & _____

www.pentopaperpublishing.com

How to Use this Journal

No two couples are alike and therefore no two Bucket Lists will be alike. Your list is as unique as you are.

When people think of Bucket Lists, very often there's a temptation just to write down exotic locations with sun-kissed beaches, sipping cocktails, being waited on hand and foot while staying at the best five star hotels – and there is nothing wrong with that.

If it motivates you to get creative on how you're going to achieve it and plan your life accordingly, then all to the good. Go for it. That said, if achieving your Bucket List is reliant on having millions in the bank, unless you're super rich, there may not be many items getting ticked off as done. It's important to remember that building a lifetime of memories is not dependant on spending huge sums of money. There is as much joy in the little things so don't forget to have them on your list

The beauty of creating your list as a couple is that you already have something which you can't put a value on – each other. You can share your adventures with the person who means the most to you which give new meaning and joy to the ordinary as well as the extraordinary.

While going through the process of putting a list together, you may also find out thing about each other that you didn't know which makes this all the more exciting.

Did you know that as a child your partner dreamed of sleeping beneath the stars with a camp fire blazing for warmth? Wouldn't that be wonderful to make their dream come true? Or that you always wanted to try Tai food? Well you could put on your list to go to Taiwan (and why not) or you could find a restaurant closer to home and make it a special occasion.

Perhaps you're an animal lover. If so, how awesome would it be for you to both volunteer for a day at the local rescue centre? It could just be that some of the best things in life actually are free.

The message is to really think about what truly makes you happy. If there are big things on the list, that's fantastic. Don't leave them off because you think they may be beyond your reach. If they are important to you, together you'll find a way.

Make it your mission to ensure you do. At the end of the day, we only come this way once. But don't forget what some may consider the little things. If they are important to you and you achieve them, how much richer your life will be.

The best thing to do is chunk it all down: big, small, crazy, bazaar, close to home or on distant shores – it doesn't matter, as long as it's something you want to do for you.

Sure there may be some compromises along the way, but that's part of the fun, part of the learning experience and part of bringing you together as a couple.

Enjoy and let your spirits run free. This is your time so don't waste a moment.

Using the Bucket List Ideas

Included in this journal is a list of ideas. Some you may think are great and things that you want to include on your list but their main purpose is to act as prompts to get your creative juices flowing.

If for example, one on the prompts suggests taking up a sport together and the idea of trudging round a golf course for four hours is you partners idea of a living hell – what can you do? It could be something like Taekwondo which is amazing for the mind, body and soul.

The important thing here is to perhaps be inspired by the list of ideas but to make yours even better by personalizing to just for you. To help there are also the **brainstorming pages**.

Take some quiet time together and play with them. By the time you finish with these pages they should look like a crazy spider. There should be no filters - that can come later. For now just write down whatever comes to mind. Don't over think it, there are no barriers.

Next, choose your top 50 Bucket List Items - and what a list that will be. Go for some quick wins to get the momentum going. Perhaps things you can do close to home and intersperse them with some of the bigger items on your list.

On the individual list pages, there is a section on what you have to do to make it happen. Start thinking about that now. They are going to happen, you just need to figure out how.

Let the adventures begin.

"Stop dreaming about your bucket list and start living it."
Annette White

Item	Description	When	Tick
1			
2			
3			
4			
5			
6			
7			
8			
9			
10			
11			
12			
13			
14			
15			
16			
17			

Item	Description	When	Tick
18			
19			
20			
21			
22			
23			
24			
25			
26			
27			
28			
29			
30			
31			
32			
33			
34			

Item	Description	When	Tick
35			
36			
37			
38			
39			
40			
41			
42			
43			
44			
45			
46			
47			
48			
49			
50			

01 _____

We want this because _____

_____

_____

To make this happen we need to _____

_____

_____

Adventure Awaits - Let's Do This

*Date Completed*_____ *Location*_____

*Our Story*_____

_____

_____

_____

_____

_____

*The Best Part*_____

_____

_____

_____

*What We Learned*_____

_____

_____

_____

Other stuff we want to remember _____

_____

_____

_____

_____

_____

_____

Stick or draw things here

02

We want this because _____
_____
_____

To make this happen we need to _____
_____
_____

Adventure Awaits - Let's do this

*Date Completed*_____ *Location*_____

*Our Story*_____
_____
_____
_____
_____

*The Best Part*_____
_____
_____
_____

*What We Learned*_____
_____
_____
_____

Other stuff we want to remember _____

_____

_____

_____

_____

_____

_____

Stick or draw things here

03

We want this because _____
_____
_____

To make this happen we need to _____
_____
_____

Adventure Awaits - Let's do this

*Date Completed*_____ *Location*_____

*Our Story*_____
_____
_____
_____
_____
_____

*The Best Part*_____
_____
_____
_____

*What We Learned*_____
_____
_____
_____

Other stuff we want to remember _____

_____

_____

_____

_____

_____

_____

Stick or draw things here

04

We want this because _____

_____

_____

To make this happen we need to _____

_____

_____

Adventure Awaits - Let's do this

*Date Completed*_____ *Location*_____

*Our Story*_____

_____

_____

_____

_____

_____

*The Best Part*_____

_____

_____

_____

*What We Learned*_____

_____

_____

_____

Other stuff we want to remember _____

_____

_____

_____

_____

_____

_____

Stick or draw things here

05

We want this because _____

_____

_____

To make this happen we need to _____

_____

_____

Adventure Awaits - Let's do this

*Date Completed*_____ *Location*_____

*Our Story*_____

_____

_____

_____

_____

*The Best Part*_____

_____

_____

_____

*What We Learned*_____

_____

_____

_____

Other stuff we want to remember _____

_____

_____

_____

_____

_____

_____

Stick or draw things here

06 _____

We want this because _____
_____
_____

To make this happen we need to _____
_____
_____

Adventure Awaits - Let's do this

*Date Completed*_____ *Location*_____

*Our Story*_____
_____
_____
_____
_____
_____

*The Best Part*_____
_____
_____
_____

*What We Learned*_____
_____
_____
_____

Other stuff we want to remember _____

_____

_____

_____

_____

_____

_____

Stick or draw things here

07 _____
_____

We want this because _____
_____
_____

To make this happen we need to _____
_____
_____

Adventure Awaits - Let's do this

*Date Completed*_____ *Location*_____

*Our Story*_____
_____
_____
_____
_____
_____

*The Best Part*_____
_____
_____
_____

*What We Learned*_____
_____
_____
_____

Other stuff we want to remember _____

_____

_____

_____

_____

_____

_____

Stick or draw things here

08 _____
_____

We want this because _____
_____
_____

To make this happen we need to _____
_____
_____

Adventure Awaits - Let's do this

*Date Completed*_____ *Location*_____

*Our Story*_____
_____
_____
_____
_____
_____

*The Best Part*_____
_____
_____
_____

*What We Learned*_____
_____
_____
_____

Other stuff we want to remember _____

_____

_____

_____

_____

_____

_____

Stick or draw things here

09
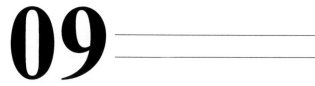

We want this because _____
_____
_____

To make this happen we need to _____
_____
_____

Adventure Awaits - Let's do this

*Date Completed*_____ *Location*_____

*Our Story*_____
_____
_____
_____
_____
_____

*The Best Part*_____
_____
_____
_____

*What We Learned*_____
_____
_____
_____

Other stuff we want to remember _____

_____

_____

_____

_____

_____

_____

Stick or draw things here

10 _____
_____

We want this because _____
_____
_____

To make this happen we need to _____
_____
_____

Adventure Awaits - Let's do this

*Date Completed*_____ *Location*_____

*Our Story*_____
_____
_____
_____
_____
_____

*The Best Part*_____
_____
_____
_____

*What We Learned*_____
_____
_____
_____

Other stuff we want to remember _____

_____

_____

_____

_____

_____

_____

Stick or draw things here

11 _____
_____

We want this because _____
_____
_____

To make this happen we need to _____
_____
_____

Adventure Awaits - Let's do this

*Date Completed*_____ *Location*_____

*Our Story*_____
_____
_____
_____
_____
_____

*The Best Part*_____
_____
_____
_____

*What We Learned*_____
_____
_____
_____

Other stuff we want to remember _____

_____

_____

_____

_____

_____

_____

Stick or draw things here

12 _____

We want this because _____

_____

_____

To make this happen we need to _____

_____

_____

Adventure Awaits - Let's do this

*Date Completed*_____ *Location*_____

*Our Story*_____

_____

_____

_____

_____

_____

*The Best Part*_____

_____

_____

_____

*What We Learned*_____

_____

_____

_____

Other stuff we want to remember _____

_____

_____

_____

_____

_____

_____

Stick or draw things here

13 _____
_____

We want this because _____
_____
_____

To make this happen we need to _____
_____
_____

Adventure Awaits - Let's do this

*Date Completed*_____ *Location*_____

*Our Story*_____
_____
_____
_____
_____
_____

*The Best Part*_____
_____
_____
_____

*What We Learned*_____
_____
_____
_____

Other stuff we want to remember _____

_____

_____

_____

_____

_____

_____

Stick or draw things here

14 _____
_____

We want this because _____
_____
_____

To make this happen we need to _____
_____
_____

Adventure Awaits - Let's do this

*Date Completed*_____ *Location*_____

*Our Story*_____
_____
_____
_____
_____
_____

*The Best Part*_____
_____
_____
_____

*What We Learned*_____
_____
_____
_____

Other stuff we want to remember _____

_____

_____

_____

_____

_____

_____

Stick or draw things here

15 _____

_____

We want this because _____

_____

_____

To make this happen we need to _____

_____

_____

Adventure Awaits - Let's do this

_Date Completed_____ _Location_____

_Our Story_____

_____

_____

_____

_____

_____

_The Best Part_____

_____

_____

_____

_What We Learned_____

_____

_____

_____

Other stuff we want to remember _____

_____

_____

_____

_____

_____

_____

Stick or draw things here

16 _____

We want this because _____
_____
_____

To make this happen we need to _____
_____
_____

Adventure Awaits - Let's do this

_Date Completed_____ _Location_____

_Our Story_____
_____
_____
_____
_____
_____

_The Best Part_____
_____
_____
_____

_What We Learned_____
_____
_____
_____

Other stuff we want to remember _____

_____

_____

_____

_____

_____

_____

Stick or draw things here

17

We want this because _____
_____
_____

To make this happen we need to _____
_____
_____

Adventure Awaits - Let's do this

Date Completed_____ Location_____

Our Story_____
_____
_____
_____
_____
_____

The Best Part_____
_____
_____
_____

What We Learned_____
_____
_____
_____

Other stuff we want to remember _____

_____

_____

_____

_____

_____

_____

Stick or draw things here

18 _____
_____

We want this because _____
_____
_____

To make this happen we need to _____
_____
_____

Adventure Awaits - Let's do this

Date Completed _____ *Location* _____

Our Story _____
_____
_____
_____
_____
_____

The Best Part _____
_____
_____
_____

What We Learned _____
_____
_____
_____

Other stuff we want to remember _____

_____

_____

_____

_____

_____

_____

Stick or draw things here

19

We want this because _____

_____

_____

To make this happen we need to _____

_____

_____

Adventure Awaits - Let's do this

Date Completed_____ Location_____

Our Story_____

_____

_____

_____

_____

_____

The Best Part_____

_____

_____

_____

What We Learned_____

_____

_____

_____

Other stuff we want to remember _____

_____

_____

_____

_____

_____

_____

Stick or draw things here

20 ───────────

We want this because _____
_____
_____

To make this happen we need to _____
_____
_____

Adventure Awaits - Let's do this

*Date Completed*_____ *Location*_____

*Our Story*_____
_____
_____
_____
_____

*The Best Part*_____
_____
_____
_____

*What We Learned*_____
_____
_____
_____

Other stuff we want to remember _____

_____

_____

_____

_____

_____

_____

Stick or draw things here

21

_____

_____

We want this because _____

_____

_____

To make this happen we need to _____

_____

_____

Adventure Awaits - Let's do this

_Date Completed_____ _Location_____

_Our Story_____

_____

_____

_____

_____

_____

_The Best Part_____

_____

_____

_____

_What We Learned_____

_____

_____

_____

Other stuff we want to remember _____

_____

_____

_____

_____

_____

_____

Stick or draw things here

22 _____
_____

We want this because _____
_____
_____

To make this happen we need to _____
_____
_____

Adventure Awaits - Let's do this

*Date Completed*_____ *Location*_____

*Our Story*_____
_____
_____
_____
_____
_____

*The Best Part*_____
_____
_____
_____

*What We Learned*_____
_____
_____
_____

Other stuff we want to remember _____

_____

_____

_____

_____

_____

Stick or draw things here

23 _____
_____

We want this because _____
_____
_____

To make this happen we need to _____
_____
_____

Adventure Awaits - Let's do this

*Date Completed*_____ *Location*_____

*Our Story*_____
_____
_____
_____
_____
_____

*The Best Part*_____
_____
_____
_____

*What We Learned*_____
_____
_____
_____

Other stuff we want to remember _____

_____
_____
_____
_____
_____
_____

Stick or draw things here

24 _____

We want this because _____
_____
_____

To make this happen we need to _____
_____
_____

Adventure Awaits - Let's do this

*Date Completed*_____ *Location*_____

*Our Story*_____
_____
_____
_____
_____
_____

*The Best Part*_____
_____
_____
_____

*What We Learned*_____
_____
_____
_____

Other stuff we want to remember _____

_____

_____

_____

_____

_____

_____

Stick or draw things here

25 _____

We want this because _____
_____
_____

To make this happen we need to _____
_____
_____

Adventure Awaits - Let's do this

_Date Completed_____ _Location_____

_Our Story_____
_____
_____
_____
_____
_____

_The Best Part_____
_____
_____
_____

_What We Learned_____
_____
_____
_____

Other stuff we want to remember _____

_____

_____

_____

_____

_____

_____

Stick or draw things here

26 _____

We want this because _____
_____
_____

To make this happen we need to _____
_____
_____

Adventure Awaits - Let's do this

*Date Completed*_____ *Location*_____

*Our Story*_____
_____
_____
_____
_____
_____

*The Best Part*_____
_____
_____
_____

*What We Learned*_____
_____
_____
_____

Other stuff we want to remember _____

_____

_____

_____

_____

_____

_____

Stick or draw things here

27 _____
_____

We want this because _____
_____
_____

To make this happen we need to _____
_____
_____

Adventure Awaits - Let's do this

*Date Completed*_____ *Location*_____

*Our Story*_____
_____
_____
_____
_____
_____

*The Best Part*_____
_____
_____
_____

*What We Learned*_____
_____
_____
_____

Other stuff we want to remember _____

_____
_____
_____
_____
_____
_____

Stick or draw things here

28

We want this because _____

_____

_____

To make this happen we need to _____

_____

_____

Adventure Awaits - Let's do this

_Date Completed_____ _Location_____

_Our Story_____

_____

_____

_____

_____

_____

_The Best Part_____

_____

_____

_____

_What We Learned_____

_____

_____

_____

Other stuff we want to remember _____

_____

_____

_____

_____

_____

_____

Stick or draw things here

29 _____

We want this because _____
_____
_____

To make this happen we need to _____
_____
_____

Adventure Awaits - Let's do this

*Date Completed*_____ *Location*_____

*Our Story*_____
_____
_____
_____
_____
_____

*The Best Part*_____
_____
_____
_____

*What We Learned*_____
_____
_____
_____

Other stuff we want to remember _____

_____

_____

_____

_____

_____

_____

Stick or draw things here

30 _____
_____

We want this because _____
_____
_____

To make this happen we need to _____
_____
_____

Adventure Awaits - Let's do this

*Date Completed*_____ *Location*_____

*Our Story*_____
_____
_____
_____
_____
_____

*The Best Part*_____
_____
_____
_____

*What We Learned*_____
_____
_____
_____

Other stuff we want to remember _____

_____

_____

_____

_____

_____

_____

Stick or draw things here

31

We want this because _____

_____

_____

To make this happen we need to _____

_____

_____

Adventure Awaits - Let's do this

Date Completed_____ Location_____

Our Story_____

_____

_____

_____

_____

_____

The Best Part_____

_____

_____

_____

What We Learned_____

_____

_____

_____

Other stuff we want to remember _____

_____

_____

_____

_____

_____

_____

Stick or draw things here

32 _____
_____

We want this because _____
_____
_____

To make this happen we need to _____
_____
_____

Adventure Awaits - Let's do this

*Date Completed*_____ *Location*_____

*Our Story*_____
_____
_____
_____
_____
_____

*The Best Part*_____
_____
_____
_____

*What We Learned*_____
_____
_____
_____

Other stuff we want to remember _____

_____

_____

_____

_____

_____

_____

Stick or draw things here

33 _____
_____

We want this because _____
_____
_____

To make this happen we need to _____
_____
_____

Adventure Awaits - Let's do this

*Date Completed*_____ *Location*_____

*Our Story*_____
_____
_____
_____
_____
_____

*The Best Part*_____
_____
_____
_____

*What We Learned*_____
_____
_____
_____

Other stuff we want to remember _____

_____

_____

_____

_____

_____

_____

Stick or draw things here

34

We want this because _____
_____
_____

To make this happen we need to _____
_____
_____

Adventure Awaits - Let's do this

Date Completed_____ Location_____

Our Story_____
_____
_____
_____
_____
_____

The Best Part_____
_____
_____
_____

What We Learned_____
_____
_____
_____

Other stuff we want to remember _____

_____

_____

_____

_____

_____

_____

Stick or draw things here

35 _____
_____

We want this because _____
_____
_____

To make this happen we need to _____
_____
_____

Adventure Awaits - Let's do this

*Date Completed*_____ *Location*_____

*Our Story*_____
_____
_____
_____
_____
_____

*The Best Part*_____
_____
_____
_____

*What We Learned*_____
_____
_____
_____

Other stuff we want to remember _____

_____

_____

_____

_____

_____

_____

Stick or draw things here

36

We want this because _____

_____

_____

To make this happen we need to _____

_____

_____

Adventure Awaits - Let's do this

Date Completed_____ Location_____

Our Story_____

_____

_____

_____

_____

_____

The Best Part_____

_____

_____

_____

What We Learned_____

_____

_____

_____

Other stuff we want to remember _____

_____

_____

_____

_____

_____

_____

Stick or draw things here

37 _____
_____

We want this because _____
_____
_____

To make this happen we need to _____
_____
_____

Adventure Awaits - Let's do this

*Date Completed*_____ *Location*_____

*Our Story*_____
_____
_____
_____
_____
_____

*The Best Part*_____
_____
_____
_____

*What We Learned*_____
_____
_____
_____

Other stuff we want to remember _____

_____

_____

_____

_____

_____

_____

Stick or draw things here

38

We want this because _____
_____
_____

To make this happen we need to _____
_____
_____

Adventure Awaits - Let's do this

Date Completed_____ Location_____

Our Story_____
_____
_____
_____
_____
_____

The Best Part_____
_____
_____
_____

What We Learned_____
_____
_____
_____

Other stuff we want to remember _____

_____

_____

_____

_____

_____

Stick or draw things here

39 _____

We want this because _____
_____
_____

To make this happen we need to _____
_____
_____

Adventure Awaits - Let's do this

_Date Completed_____ _Location_____

_Our Story_____
_____
_____
_____
_____
_____

_The Best Part_____
_____
_____
_____

_What We Learned_____
_____
_____
_____

Other stuff we want to remember _____

_____

_____

_____

_____

_____

_____

Stick or draw things here

40

We want this because _____

_____

_____

To make this happen we need to _____

_____

_____

Adventure Awaits - Let's do this

*Date Completed*_____ *Location*_____

*Our Story*_____

_____

_____

_____

_____

_____

*The Best Part*_____

_____

_____

_____

*What We Learned*_____

_____

_____

_____

Other stuff we want to remember _____

_____

_____

_____

_____

_____

_____

Stick or draw things here

41

We want this because _____
_____
_____

To make this happen we need to _____
_____
_____

Adventure Awaits - Let's do this

_Date Completed_____ _Location_____

_Our Story_____
_____
_____
_____
_____
_____

_The Best Part_____
_____
_____
_____

_What We Learned_____
_____
_____
_____

Other stuff we want to remember _____

_____

_____

_____

_____

_____

_____

Stick or draw things here

42

We want this because _____

_____

_____

To make this happen we need to _____

_____

_____

Adventure Awaits - Let's do this

*Date Completed*_____ *Location*_____

*Our Story*_____

_____

_____

_____

_____

*The Best Part*_____

_____

_____

_____

*What We Learned*_____

_____

_____

_____

Other stuff we want to remember _____

_____

_____

_____

_____

_____

_____

Stick or draw things here

43

We want this because _____

_____

_____

To make this happen we need to _____

_____

_____

Adventure Awaits - Let's do this

*Date Completed*_____ *Location*_____

*Our Story*_____

_____

_____

_____

_____

_____

*The Best Part*_____

_____

_____

_____

*What We Learned*_____

_____

_____

_____

Other stuff we want to remember _____

_____

_____

_____

_____

_____

_____

Stick or draw things here

44

We want this because _____
_____
_____

To make this happen we need to _____
_____
_____

Adventure Awaits - Let's do this

*Date Completed*_____ *Location*_____

*Our Story*_____
_____
_____
_____
_____

*The Best Part*_____
_____
_____
_____

*What We Learned*_____
_____
_____
_____

Other stuff we want to remember _____

_____
_____
_____
_____
_____
_____

Stick or draw things here

45

We want this because _____

_____

_____

To make this happen we need to _____

_____

_____

Adventure Awaits - Let's do this

*Date Completed*_____ *Location*_____

*Our Story*_____

_____

_____

_____

_____

_____

*The Best Part*_____

_____

_____

_____

*What We Learned*_____

_____

_____

_____

Other stuff we want to remember _____

_____

_____

_____

_____

_____

_____

Stick or draw things here

46

We want this because _____
_____
_____

To make this happen we need to _____
_____
_____

Adventure Awaits - Let's do this

*Date Completed*_____ *Location*_____

*Our Story*_____
_____
_____
_____
_____
_____

*The Best Part*_____
_____
_____
_____

*What We Learned*_____
_____
_____
_____

Other stuff we want to remember _____

_____

_____

_____

_____

_____

_____

Stick or draw things here

47

We want this because _____
_____
_____

To make this happen we need to _____
_____
_____

Adventure Awaits - Let's do this

Date Completed_____ Location_____

Our Story_____
_____
_____
_____
_____
_____

The Best Part_____
_____
_____
_____

What We Learned_____
_____
_____
_____

Other stuff we want to remember _____

_____

_____

_____

_____

_____

_____

Stick or draw things here

48

We want this because _____
_____
_____

To make this happen we need to _____
_____
_____

Adventure Awaits - Let's do this

*Date Completed*_____ *Location*_____

*Our Story*_____
_____
_____
_____
_____
_____

*The Best Part*_____
_____
_____
_____

*What We Learned*_____
_____
_____
_____

Other stuff we want to remember _____

_____

_____

_____

_____

_____

_____

Stick or draw things here

49

We want this because _____
_____
_____

To make this happen we need to _____
_____
_____

Adventure Awaits - Let's do this

*Date Completed*_____ *Location*_____

*Our Story*_____
_____
_____
_____
_____
_____

*The Best Part*_____
_____
_____
_____

*What We Learned*_____
_____
_____
_____

Other stuff we want to remember _____

_____
_____
_____
_____
_____
_____

Stick or draw things here

50 _____
_____

We want this because _____
_____
_____

To make this happen we need to _____
_____
_____

Adventure Awaits - Let's do this

Date Completed _____ *Location* _____

Our Story _____
_____
_____
_____
_____
_____

The Best Part _____
_____
_____
_____

What We Learned _____
_____
_____
_____

Other stuff we want to remember _____

_____

_____

_____

_____

_____

_____

Stick or draw things here

Notes

Notes

Notes

Places we'd like to go.

Things we'd like to do.

Things we'd like to learn.

Things we'd like to achieve.

Things we'd like to have.

Random stuff.

Bucket List Ideas.

Places we'd like to go.

- ✓ Visit Paris in the Springtime.
- ✓ Take a gondola ride in Venice.
- ✓ See the sun rise ay Machu Picchu.
- ✓ Hike the Grand Canyon.
- ✓ Go whale watching in Alaska.
- ✓ Bring in the New Year in Edinburgh, Scotland.
- ✓ Tour the Italian Lakes.
- ✓ Dance at the Samba Carnival in Rio.
- ✓ Experience the Northern Lights in Finland.
- ✓ Visit every landmark in your town or city.
- ✓ Cruise the Nile.
- ✓ See the Coliseum in Rome.
- ✓ Stay in an ice hotel in Sweden.

Things we'd like to do.

- ✓ See a West End or Broadway show.
- ✓ Go to Disney Land and be kids again.
- ✓ Get ticket to see your favorite band in concert.
- ✓ Take a helicopter of hot air balloon ride.
- ✓ Go backpacking.
- ✓ Dine in a Michelin Star restaurant.
- ✓ Name a star.
- ✓ Have a night at the opera.
- ✓ Perform random acts of kindness.
- ✓ Go paintballing.
- ✓ Run a 5k together.
- ✓ Sleep under the stars.
- ✓ Volunteer for a local charity.
- ✓ Go to a major sporting event.
- ✓ Watch the sun rise and set in one day.
- ✓ Go camping or glamping.
- ✓ Have a technology free day.
- ✓ Re-model a room in your home using only refurbished items.

Bucket List Ideas.

Things we'd like to learn.

✓ Learn a new language.
✓ Pick up a musical instrument.
✓ Try a new sport.
✓ Book on a cookery course.
✓ Take ballroom or salsa dancing classes.
✓ Learn to scuba dive.
✓ How to brew you own beer or wine (or both.)
✓ Take a photography class.
✓ Find your nearest dry sky slope and book a taster session.
✓ Join a yoga class.
✓ Study the art of meditation.
✓ Take a class in basic home repairs at your local college.
✓ Learn first aid.

Things we'd like to achieve.

✓ Design and build your own home.
✓ Live in a different country.
✓ Face your biggest fears as a team.
✓ Create a plan to become debt free.
✓ Start a business to help fund your adventures.
✓ Study for a new qualification.
✓ Have new career.
✓ Take your parents or close friends on vacation.
✓ Buy a holiday home on the coast.
✓ Create a decluttered life to make your home restful and inspiring.
✓ Write a mission statement for you as a couple.
✓ Make a new family tradition that you can look forward to every year.

Pen To Paper Publishing title for you to enjoy:

The Gratitude Habit Journal

"When you are grateful, fear disappears and abundance appears." –
Anthony Robbins

The Gratitude Habit is a 100 Day Journal specially designed to help to
capture the important things in your life for which you are grateful. It
doesn't matter if it's something big or small but what's important is that you
write them down, reflect on and fully enjoy them.

This Journal is Unique to You. As soon as you put pen to paper this
gratitude journal becomes unique - there will never be another like it.
Journaling twice a day is found to be most beneficial - first thing in the
morning and last thing at night.

What better way to start your day happy and end your day contented.

The title is available exclusively on Amazon. Just type this link into your
browser:

Bit.ly/GratitudeHabitJournal

Passwords Melt My Brain

**Does trying to remember your logins, usernames and passwords Melt
Your Brain?**

With the need for internet passwords to be more and more complicated, the
chances of remember them all becomes a real challenge. So what happens
in you forget one? Well, you have to submit a request to the website hosts,
they email you, you ten have to log on again, create a new password, have
that accepted……..by now you're in Brain Melt City Arizona. And you've
spent a whole bunch of time getting there.

This password keeper offers a simple solution – all you important website
addresses, usernames and passwords logged in one convenient place.

To find this title on Amazon, type this link into your browser:

Bit.ly/PasswordsMeltMyBrain

amazon.com/author/pentopaper

Made in the USA
San Bernardino, CA
27 December 2019